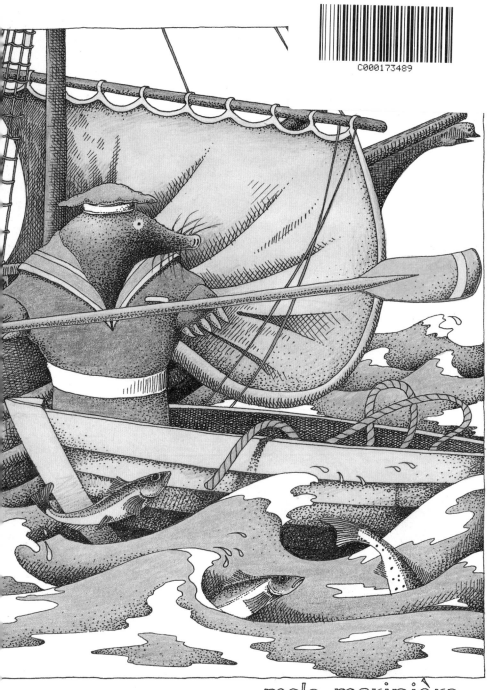

mole marinière

SIMON DREW'S
BIRTHDAY BOOK

TWO MERRY COOKS
SPOILING THE BROTH

SIMON DREW'S
BIRTHDAY BOOK

sweet
f. a.

ANTIQUE COLLECTORS' CLUB

to Caroline
and to Carol and Tina
and to Sue, Abi and Bronwyn
who all have birthdays

HENGEHOGS

ISBN 978 190537 761 9

British Library Cataloguing-in-Publication Data
A catalogue record for this book is available from the British Library

Printed in China for the Antique Collectors' Club Ltd.,
Woodbridge, Suffolk, England

HEAD COOK
& BOTTLE WATCHER

I drive way too fast
to worry
about cholesterol

jan 1

_____ aardvark day

jan 4

_____ tarantula day

jan 2

_____ sole day

jan 5

_____ albatross day

jan 3

_____ abalone day

jan 6

trapdoor spider day

jan 8

____squid day

jan 9

____alligator day

jan 7

____krill day

jan 10

____starfish day

jan 11

_____ amoeba day

jan 13

_____ anaconda day

jan 12

_____ stick insect day

jan 14

_____ clam day

CAPTAIN COOK

AQUARIUS
january 20 to february 18

Aquarians know how to find
the way to your heart: they're so
kind.
When two of them meet
it's amazingly sweet:
like two growing vines intertwined.

jan 15

_____ anemone day

jan 18

_____ swordfish day

jan 16

_____ shoveler duck day

jan 19

_____ antelope day

jan 17

_____ angelfish day

jan 20

_____ spoonbill day

jan 21

anteater day

jan 24

corncrake day

jan 22

bittern day

jan 25

aphid day

jan 23

ant day

jan 26

terrapin day

jan 27

archaeopteryx day

WIMBLEDOG

jan 28

tiger day

jan 30

tigerfish day

jan 29

armadillo day

jan 31

auk day

feb 1

_____ axolotl day

feb 4

_____ tortoise day

feb 2

_____ toad day

feb 5

_____ barnacle day

feb 3

_____ baboon day

feb 6

_____ trilobite day

feb 7

barracuda day

feb 9

bat day

feb 8

trout day

feb 10

tuna day

curious cat with tooth hake

feb 11

bath sponge day

feb 14

vulture day

feb 12

turtle day

feb 15

beaver day

feb 13

black bear day

feb 16

wallaby day

the dance of the seven whales

feb 17

‗bumblebee day

feb 18

‗walrus day

PISCES
february 19 to march 20

Pisceans are meant to like water:
they dive in like lambs to the
slaughter.
If tepid or cool,
please show them a pool:
they're just like a whale, only shorter.

feb 19

_____ honey bee day

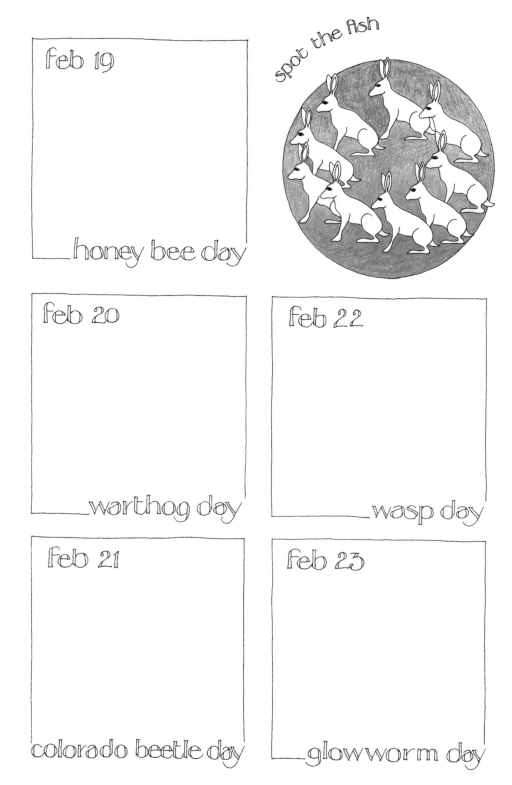

feb 20

_____ warthog day

feb 22

_____ wasp day

feb 21

colorado beetle day

feb 23

_____ glowworm day

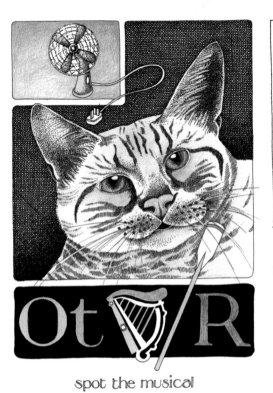

spot the musical

feb 25

whirligig beetle day

feb 26

blue whale day

feb 24

waxbill day

feb 27

beluga day

cleanliness is next to dogliness

feb 28

woodpecker day

feb 29

bird of paradise day

mar 1

bream day

mar 2

fin whale day

mar 3

buffalo day

mar 4

right whale day

mar 5

bullfrog day

mar 6

killer whale day

ACE OF PUFFINS (WITH SEAFOOD)

mar 7

bush cricket day

mar 10

yellowhammer day

mar 8

woodpigeon day

mar 11

tortoiseshell day

mar 9

butterfly day

mar 12

zebra day

There aint nothing like a Dane

mar 13

red admiral day

mar 14

avocet day

mar 15

butterfly fish day

mar 16

bantam day

mar 17

cabbage white day

ARIES
march 21 to april 19

People in Aries are strong
and their memories never seem wrong.
They're fond of a dance
and, given a chance,
they'll suddenly burst into song.

mar 18

blackbird day

mar 21

capybara day

mar 19

camel day

mar 22

bullfinch day

mar 20

budgerigar day

mar 23

carp day

mar 24

bunting day

mar 27

catfish day

mar 25

cassowary day

mar 28

buzzard day

mar 26

bustard day

mar 29

cat day

tails of the riverbank

drew

mar 30	mar 31
capercaillie day	centipede day

apr 1

chameleon day

apr 2

chaffinch day

apr 3

chicken day

apr 4

chiffchaff day

apr 5

chimpanzee day

apr 6

chough day

apr 7

cobra day

apr 8

cormorant day

Elgin's cat playing with his marbles

apr 9

cockle day

apr 12

crossbill day

apr 10

crane day

apr 13

condor day

apr 11

coelocanth day

apr 14

crow day

a problem shared is gossip

apr 15	apr 16
coral day	curlew day

TAURUS

april 20 to may 20

People from Taurus will smile
and make all your thoughts seem
worthwhile
and, though not a sin,
they're fond of a gin
and their fashion is always in style.

apr 17

crab day

apr 20

cocker spaniel day

apr 18

dodo day

apr 21

crocodile day

apr 19

crayfish day

apr 22

airedale terrier day

apr 23

cuckoo day

apr 26

basset hound day

apr 24

dingo day

apr 27

damsel fly day

apr 25

cuttlefish day

apr 28

bloodhound day

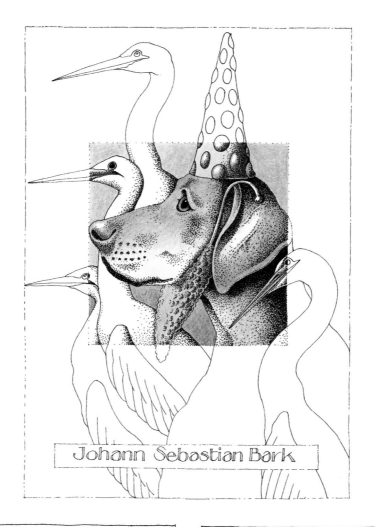

Johann Sebastian Bark

apr 29

dogfish day

apr 30

border collie day

may 1

dolphin day

may 2

boxer day

may 3

dove day

may 4

bull terrier day

When shall we three eat again?

may 5

dragonfly day

may 6

bulldog day

may 7

dromedary day

may 8

cairn terrier day

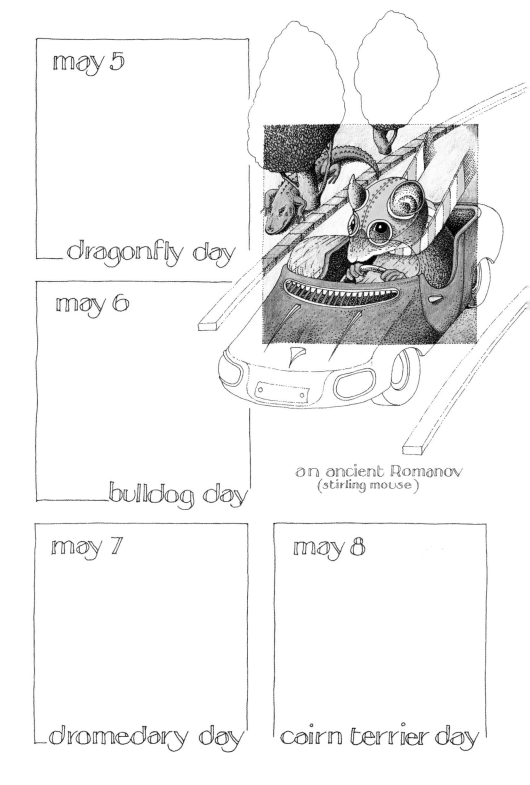

an ancient Romanov
(stirling mouse)

may 9

mallard day

may 12

corgi day

may 10

chihuahua day

may 13

eagle day

may 11

bass day

may 14

dachshund day

GREEN PEACE

may 15

earthworm day

may 16

dalmatian day

GEMINI
may 21 to june 21

Gemini must be the sign
for those with a liking for wine;
and they'll sing you a song
that is tender and strong
that will tingle a chill down your spine.

may 17

_____earwig day

may 20

_____foxhound day

may 18

_____red setter day

may 21

_____eel day_

may 19

_____echidna day

may 22

german shepherd day

Fashion is what one
wears oneself.
Oscar Wilde

may 25

emu day

may 23

elephant day

may 26

greyhound day

may 24

golden retriever day

may 27

aye aye day

may 28

_____ husky day

may 31

_____ flying fish day

may 29

_____ flamingo day

may 30

_____ hyena day

Drag the Magic Puffin

jun 1

fox day

jun 4

jackal day

jun 2

jack russell day

jun 5

grebe day

jun 3

frog day

jun 6

labrador day

mole in one

jun 7

gecko day

jun 10

mandarin day

jun 8

runner duck day

jun 11

giraffe day

jun 9

gibbon day

jun 12

muscovy duck day

jun 13

gnu day

jun 14

ruddy duck day

If I had all the money I've spent on
drink, I'd spend it on drink.
vivian stanshall

jun 15

goby day

jun 16

white egret day

CANCER
june 22 to july 22

Cancer's the sign of a friend.
These people will give or will lend:
    they'll fetch you the moon
    but they do love a tune
and they'll sing till you go round the bend.

jun 17

goldfish day

jun 20

flycatcher day

jun 18

falcon day

jun 21

barnacle goose day

jun 19

goldfinch day

jun 22

gannet day

jun 23

gorilla day

jun 26

canada goose day

jun 24

godwit day

jun 27

guillemot day

jun 25

grasshopper day

jun 28

grouse day

Once more unto the beach
dear friends, once more.

jun 29

halibut day

jun 30

herring gull day

jul 1

_____ hare day

jul 4

pine marten day

jul 2

hen harrier day

jul 5

__ hedgehog day

jul 3

heart urchin day

jul 6

_____ weasel day

jul 7

heron day

jul 8

stoat day

a fashionable pair of
high-heeled shrews

jul 9

hippopotamus day

jul 10

pit bull terrier day

nature abhorring a vacuum

jul 11

hornet day

jul 12

poodle day

jul 13

horsefly day

jul 16

retriever day

jul 14

pug day

jul 17

hummingbird day

jul 15

housefly day

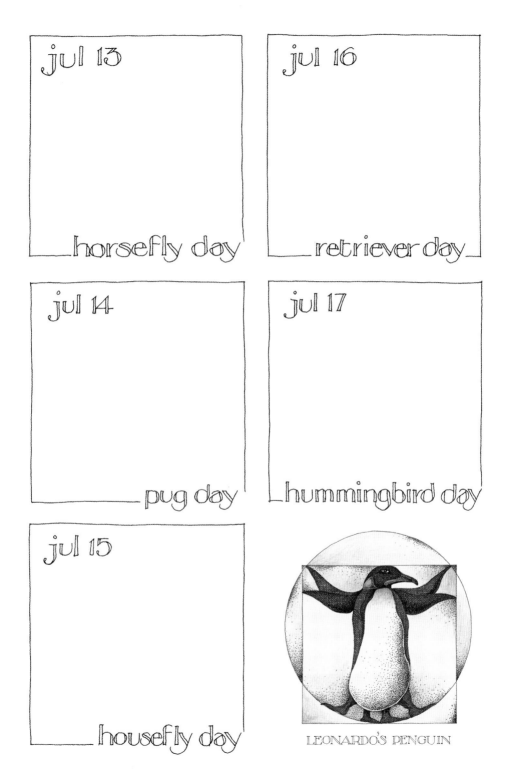

LEONARDO'S PENGUIN

LEO
july 23 to august 22

Leo is known for good looks
and people who love reading books.
This singular group
makes wonderful soup:
they're great inspirational cooks.

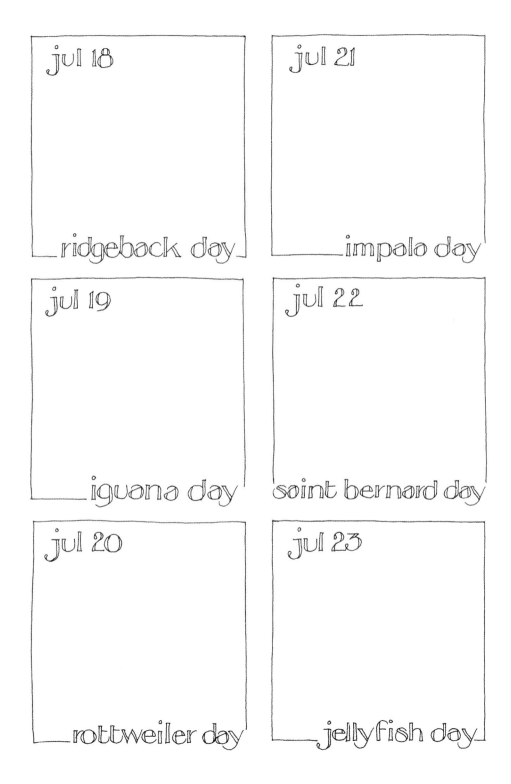

jul 18

ridgeback day

jul 19

iguana day

jul 20

rottweiler day

jul 21

impala day

jul 22

saint bernard day

jul 23

jellyfish day

jul 24

saluki day

jul 27

kingsnake day

jul 25

kangaroo day

jul 28

water spaniel day

jul 26

spaniel day

jul 29

kiwi day

BARBER QUEUE

jul 30	jul 31

springer spaniel day   koala day

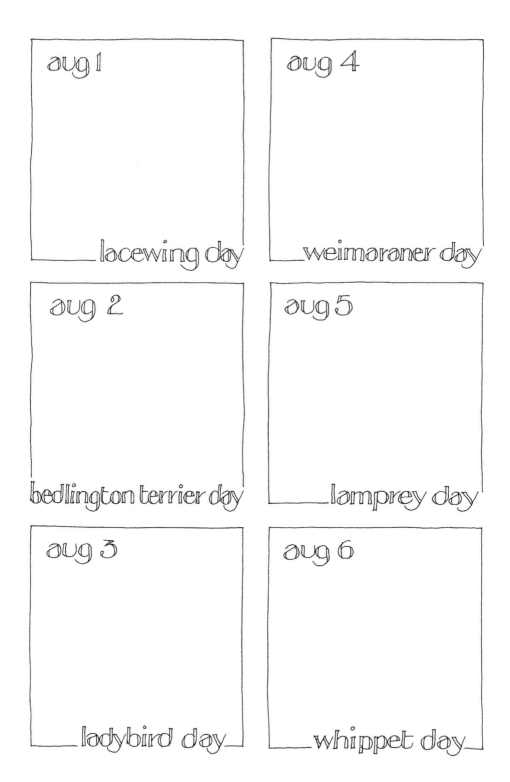

aug 1

lacewing day

aug 4

weimaraner day

aug 2

bedlington terrier day

aug 5

lamprey day

aug 3

ladybird day

aug 6

whippet day

aug 9

lion day

aug 11

lizard day

aug 10

yorkshire terrier day

aug 12

hoopoe day

HORNITHOLOGY

aug 13

llama day

aug 14

_____ ibis day

aug 15

locust day

PANTOMIME HEARSE

aug 16

jackdaw day

aug 17

lyrebird day

VIRGO
august 23 to september 22

Virgo's a sign for the daring
with people, both gentle and caring
but don't show dismay
in the heat of the day
if they throw off the clothes that
they're wearing.

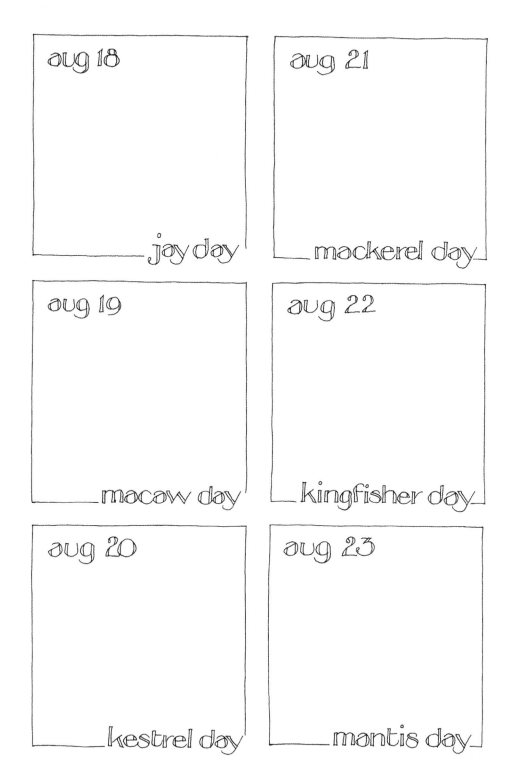

aug 18

jay day

aug 21

mackerel day

aug 19

macaw day

aug 22

kingfisher day

aug 20

kestrel day

aug 23

mantis day

aug 24

kite day

aug 26

kittiwoke day

aug 25

marsupial day

aug 27

mayfly day

"Wayne"

The moon was full as the Messerschmidt soared
and Kevin played with his parachute cord

Tracey was taking her pilot's test
and Wayne flew over the cuckoo's nest.

CAT À TONIC

with a little gin

aug 28 _____ lapwing day	aug 30 _____ lark day
aug 29 _____ millipede day	aug 31 _____ mongoose day

sep 1

monkfish day

sep 4

mosquito day

sep 2

linnet day

sep 5

moth day

sep 3

lovebird day

sep 6

magpie day

HEALTH FOOD
MAKES ME SICK

sep 7

mouse day

sep 8

house martin day

sep 9

newt day

sep 12

merlin day

sep 10

merganser day

sep 13

nightjar day

sep 11

nighthawk day

sep 14

moorhen day

GOAT CUISINE

sep 15

octopus day

sep 17

orang utan day

sep 16

nightingale day

sep 18

nutcracker day

LIBRA

september 23 to october 23

Librans are noted for brains
and a penchant for steam-driven trains
and for playing with boats;
but they never wear coats
so they get soaking wet when it rains.

sep 19

ostrich day

sep 22

osprey day

sep 20

nuthatch day

sep 23

barn owl day

sep 21

otter day

sep 24

long-eared owl day

sep 25

short-eared owl day

sep 28

partridge day

sep 26

parrot day

sep 29

sea eagle day

sep 27

tawny owl day

sep 30

peacock day

jimi hen drinks

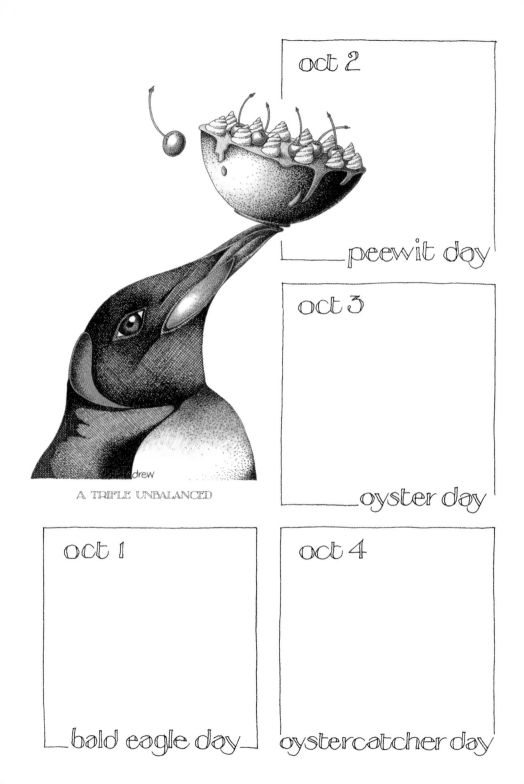

oct 2

peewit day

oct 3

oyster day

A TRIFLE UNBALANCED

oct 1

bald eagle day

oct 4

oystercatcher day

oct 5

peregrine falcon day

oct 8

pangolin day

oct 6

panda day

oct 9

pheasant day

oct 7

stormy petrel day

oct 10

pelican day

oct 11

pipit day

oct 14

ptarmigan day

oct 12

emperor penguin day

oct 15

macaroni penguin day

oct 13

king penguin day

oct 16

quail day

Corgi and Bess

oct 17

fairy penguin day

oct 18

raven day

SCORPIO

october 24 to november 21

Scorpios know how to dress:
(the rest of us look like a mess).
They sin quite a lot
though noone knows what –
they've never been known to confess

oct 19

perch day

oct 22

robin day

oct 20

ferret day

oct 23

piranha day

oct 21

pigeon day

oct 24

rook day

Only dull people are
bright at breakfast.

oct 27

platypus day

oct 25

plaice day

oct 28

shelduck day

oct 26

sandpiper day

oct 29

porcupine day

Resting under the north face of the aga

oct 30

skylark day

oct 31

puff adder day

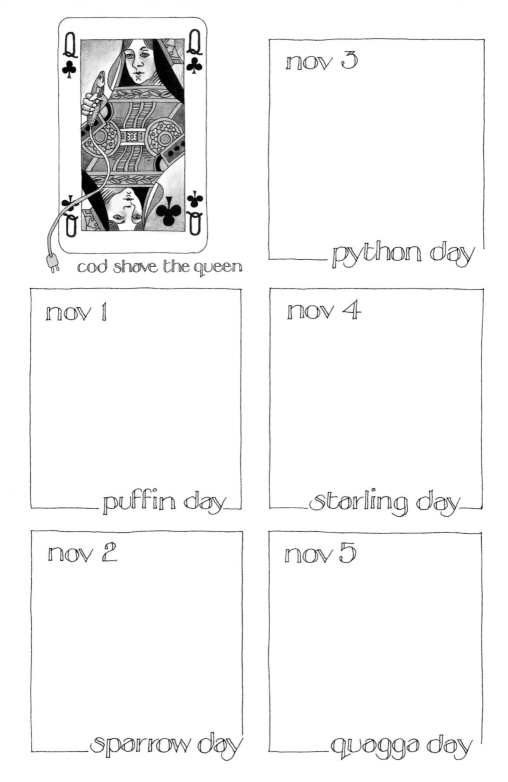

cod shave the queen

nov 3

python day

nov 1

puffin day

nov 4

starling day

nov 2

sparrow day

nov 5

quagga day

nov 6

___ swallow day

nov 7

___ rabbit day

moled wine

nov 8

___ swift day

nov 9

___ raccoon day

nov 10

_____ teal day

nov 13

_____ razorbill day

nov 11

_____ rattlesnake day

nov 14

_____ thrush day

nov 12

_____ tern day

nov 15

_____ reindeer day

poultry in motion

nov 16

blue tit day

nov 17

reptile day

SAGITTARIUS
november 22 to december 21

Sagittarians often wear pink
and will sit in the dark just to think.
You'll know who they are
in the shades of a bar
wondering which beer to drink.

nov 18

tree creeper day

nov 21

roadrunner day

nov 19

rhea day

nov 22

warbler day

nov 20

wagtail day

nov 23

salamander day

nov 24

wheatear day

nov 25

salmon day

dali havidson

nov 26

woodcock day

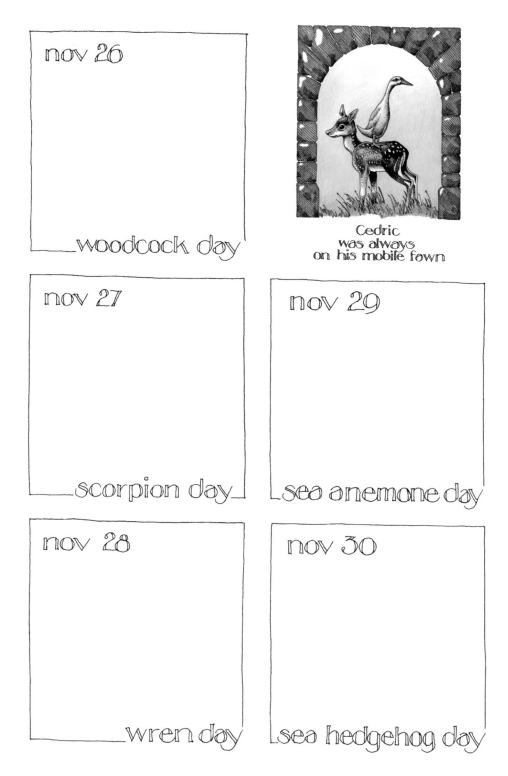

Cedric
was always
on his mobile fawn

nov 27

scorpion day

nov 29

sea anemone day

nov 28

wren day

nov 30

sea hedgehog day

dec 1

sea horse day

dec 3

sea cucumber day

dec 2

sea urchin day

dec 4

donkey day

ponchos pilot

dec 5

tiger shark day

dec 6

pig day

cat nav

dec 7

great white shark day

dec 9

shield bug day

dec 8

sheep day

dec 10

badger day

dec 11

basking shark day

dec 14

squirrel day

dec 12

deer day

dec 15

silkworm day

dec 13

shrew day

dec 16

siamese cat day

dec 17

sidewinder day

dec 18

mink day

any idiot can deal with a crisis:
it takes a genius to cope with everyday life.

CAPRICORN
december 22 to january 19

Capricorn folk never hurry:
their favourite dish is hot curry.
Then dance a few jigs
with plenty of figs.
(The effects are a bit of a worry.)

dec 19

siskin day

dec 22

woodlouse day

dec 20

lobster day

dec 23

sausage dog day

dec 21

skink day

the lion, the witch
and the fitted bedroom furniture

dec 24

sloth day

dec 25

slowworm day

dec 26

stag day

dec 27

grass snake day

dec 28

grizzly bear day

dec 29

snail day

If there wasn't an X would we care?
It's only crossed sticks in the air.
    But Xmas, I fear,
    would quite disappear:
no Santa is too much to bear.

dec 30	dec 31
polar bear day	snake day